READ WELL

UNITS 26, 27 STORYBOOK

Let Freedom Ring

ISBN 1-59318-478-6

10 09 08 07 06   3 4 5 6

SOPRIS WEST EDUCATIONAL SERVICES
A CAMBIUM LEARNING COMPANY

BOSTON, MA • LONGMONT, CO

UNIT 26 • Harriet Tubman

Follow the Star to Freedom

Planning Assistance: See Daily Lesson Planning for scheduling the Summary and Extra Practice.

UNIT 27 • Martin Luther King

Let Us Be Free

Planning Assistance: See Daily Lesson Planning for scheduling the Summary and Extra Practice.

Harriet Tubman

By Marilyn Sprick
Illustrated by Cedric Lucas

UNIT 26 STORY

Follow the Star to Freedom

Vocabulary Words

slave	moss	cart
A slave was a person who was owned by another person and made to work hard. Harriet Tubman was a slave.	Moss is a plant that grows on trees and rocks.	A cart is a wagon pulled by a horse.

---

work   working   worked

Follow the Star to Freedom

This story is about Harriet Tubman. What do you already know about Harriet? I wonder why this story is called "Follow the Star to Freedom."

CHAPTER I

When Harriet Was Little

What do you think this chapter is about?

Many years ago, thousands of black people were stolen from their homes in Africa. They were brought to the United States to be slaves. Slaves were owned by white people. Today, in the United States, no one can own another person. This story is about one slave—a real woman named Harriet Tubman.

When Harriet was little, she had to work. She had to work hard. Harriet could not rest. If she rested, she was hit. Harriet did not want to scrub, but she had to scrub. Harriet did not want to dust, but she had to dust.

Look at the picture. What is Harriet doing? What kind of jobs did Harriet have to do when she was little?

Harriet asked if she could work with the men. Harriet said, "I am strong. I can cut logs." Harriet worked with the men. She worked hard, but she wanted to be free.

At the end of this chapter, Harriet was older. Tell me two facts about Harriet.

sun　　　run　　　fun

CHAPTER 2
Working With the Men

Harriet didn't want to scrub because she wanted to work with the men. Harriet didn't want to dust because she wanted to work in the sun. She wanted to see the sky.

Harriet was strong, so she got to cut logs. She worked hard with the men. She could see the sky and feel the wind. Still, Harriet wanted to be free. So, Harriet sang as she worked, "Let us go. Let us be free."

Why did Harriet want to work with the men? What did Harriet do as she worked? What did Harriet want more than anything?

log   dog   hog

CHAPTER 3

Harriet Wants to Be Free

Harriet Tubman lived in the South. Some black people were freed by their owners, but Harriet knew that she would never be free unless she ran away. She would have to go to the North where black people were free. Harriet's father, Ben, knew that Harriet dreamed of being free.

Ben began telling Harriet things. Ben said, "Harriet, see that star in the sky. It tells us where to go."

Harriet said, "I see the star. But what if it is too dark? If I can't see the star, what should I do?"

Ben said, "Feel the moss on the trees."

Ben explained, "Moss only grows on the north side of trees. To get to the North, just follow the moss."

Who was Ben? Harriet wanted to run to freedom. Ben told her two things that would help her find her way to the North. What were they?

One day, Harriet knew it was time to go. She would follow the moss. She would follow the star.

Harriet went in the dark. She ran to the trees. She wanted to be free. It was hard, but Harriet could feel the moss and see the star.

At the end of the chapter, what did Harriet do?

CHAPTER 4

On the Run

At the end of the last chapter, Harriet ran away. What do you think happened to her?

Harriet said, "I must be free. I must."

The men sent dogs to get Harriet, but she ran. The dogs could smell Harriet, but Harriet ran in the creek. Then the dogs couldn't smell Harriet. Harriet said, "I must be free. I must."

Harriet ran in the dark. She hid on farms. She hid with friends. Harriet ran and ran until she was free. Then Harriet sang, "I am free. See me. I am free at last."

How did Harriet get away from the dogs? While she ran for freedom, Harriet had to hide. Where did she hide? What happened at the end of this chapter?

from   friend

CHAPTER 5

From Friend to Friend

Harriet Tubman was a slave who escaped to the North. She traveled along the Underground Railroad. The Underground Railroad wasn't really a railroad. It was a way to freedom. Each stop was the house of someone who wanted to help the slaves escape. When Harriet was free, she joined the Underground Railroad and began to help others escape to freedom.

Once Harriet was free, what did she do?

Harriet was free, but Tom was not.

The sun was hot, and Tom worked hard.

Still, the man was mean. He would hit Tom.

Tom wanted to be free.

Tom and Bell had kids. Bell said to Tom, "I do not want the man to sell the kids."

Tom said, "Then we must run from the man."

What did Bell tell Tom? Who wanted to be free in this story?

Tom met with Harriet. It would be hard with all the kids, but Harriet said, "Meet me when it is dark."

Why did Harriet think it would be hard for Tom and Bell to escape?

Harriet hid them in a cart. She hid them in the trees. Harriet, Tom, Bell, and the kids ran.

Where did Harriet hide Tom and Bell and their kids? I think it was very hard to escape. How do you think the kids felt?

It was a hard journey, but Harriet showed Tom, Bell, and their children how to follow the North Star. They followed the star and ran from friend to friend along the Underground Railroad.

Do you think Harriet, Bell, Tom, and the children made it to freedom?

CHAPTER 6
Free at Last

In the last chapter, who was Harriet helping? What did they want?

Harriet hid Bell, Tom, and the kids.
But Tom said, "I hear dogs!"

Harriet said, "If we run in the creek, the dogs can't smell us. The men will not get us."

Tom said, "It will be hard, but we will run fast."

Harriet said, "We will go from farm to farm. We will go from friend to friend."

At last, Harriet said, "Look! We are there."

The kids said, "We are free."

Tom and Bell said, "We are free at last!"

How do you think everyone felt when they got to freedom in the North? No one owned Tom and Bell. No one could take the children away and sell them. Can anyone do that today? Harriet Tubman helped 300 people. I think she was very brave. Who else do you think was brave?

Follow the Star to Freedom

We're going to retell
"Follow the Star to Freedom."

Look at the picture.
Who was the story about?

● At the beginning of the story,
what did Harriet have to do
when she was little?
What did she want?

■ In the middle of the story,
what did Harriet do to become free?

▲ At the end of the story,
how did Harriet help Bell, Tom,
and the kids?

This is a true story. What did we learn about Harriet Tubman?

Let's go back to the beginning and retell the whole story by looking at the
pictures. Look at the first picture. This story was about . . .

Storybook Decoding Review

■ **Sounds you know:**

f	ar	e	b	ea
I	U	m	o	a
ee	u	F	i	G

▲ **Words you can sound out:**

insects	last	feel	rest<u>ing</u>
cart	mean	rug	ask<u>ing</u>
but	fun	got	hunt<u>ing</u>

✈ **Words you have learned:**

from	could	work	one
Where	about	friends	two

✿ **Phrases you can read:**

a hard–working man   off the wall

until the end   dust and scrub

✎ **Sentences you can read:**

We must get there fast.

Harriet said, "I want to work in the sun."

Tom asked if he could go with us.

Martin Luther King

By Marilyn Sprick and Shelley V. Jones
Illustrated by Elizabeth Wolf

Let Us Be Free

Vocabulary Words

leader

A leader is a strong person others look to for help. A leader is often important.

minister

A minister is the leader in a church. A minister is a person who helps other people.

dream

A dream can be something you imagine while you are sleeping. A dream can also be something you want or wish for.

---

work   word   words

Let Us Be Free

CHAPTER I

Who Was Martin Luther King?

Who do you think this chapter is about? What do you already know about Martin Luther King?

Since the days of slavery, many people have worked to help the United States become a better place for all people to live. This story is about a man named Martin Luther King. Martin Luther King wanted all people of all colors to be treated with fairness. He wanted all people to be treated equally.

Who was Martin Luther King? Martin Luther King was a leader. He was a man with great dreams. In fact, Martin was a great man with great dreams. Martin Luther King was a hero.

A hero is a person who is very brave and helps others. I wonder why Martin Luther King became a hero. What do you wonder about Martin Luther King?

No one really knows why one man becomes a hero to us all. We think Martin's mother and father must have helped Martin become a great man. Martin Luther King's father was a Baptist minister. Martin's father taught him how to preach.

When Martin was little, he would listen to his dad. Martin's dad said that all men should be treated well.

How did Martin's father think all people should be treated? Martin's father thought all people of all colors—men, women and children—should be treated fairly.

Martin Luther King's mother was a schoolteacher. She taught Martin how to read before he went to school.

When Martin was little, he could read. He would read books with his mother, his sister, and his brother.

When Martin was a child, there were signs all over the city that said, "Whites Only." There were signs on the drinking fountains and in the restaurants. Martin couldn't drink from those fountains, and he couldn't eat in those restaurants because he was black.

Martin said, "I can read that. Why can't we drink there? Why can't we eat there?"

Martin's father and mother helped him learn that all people should be treated well. What else did Martin learn from his mother?

CHAPTER 2

Why?

In the last chapter, we learned there were signs around Martin's city that said, "Whites Only." In this chapter, Martin asks about the signs.

Martin could read when he was little. Martin said to his mother, "I can read that. We can't get a drink there. Why?"

Martin's mother nodded. "We can't get a drink there because we are black."

Then Martin said to his dad, "I can read that. We can't eat there because we are black. Why?" Martin didn't understand.

Then Martin's dad said, "We will not be free until we can eat where we want. We will not be free until we can drink where we want."

Look at Martin and his father. The sign says "Whites Only." That meant black people could not eat in that restaurant, just because they were black. Do you think that was right? I think I would be unhappy if someone told me I could not eat in a restaurant because I was too tall, too short, or the wrong color. How do you think Martin and his dad felt when they read the sign "Whites Only"?

CHAPTER 3
Martin Becomes a Leader

From a young age, Martin Luther King seemed to know what he wanted to do. By the time Martin Luther King was twenty-five, he had his doctorate and was the minister of his church.

Martin's dad was a minister. This is what Martin wanted to be too. He went to school and worked hard.

Soon Martin was a minister. As a minister Martin said, "We must treat others well, and we must be treated well."

What did Martin Luther King become? What did he tell people?

One day, a black woman named Rosa Parks was riding home on a bus. Rosa had worked all day and was tired. When a white person got on the bus, Rosa would not give up her seat. She was taken to jail. Martin thought this was wrong.

Martin said, "Rosa was not treated well." Then Martin said, "We must all be treated well. We must be free to sit where we want on a bus. We must be free."

What happened to Rosa when she wouldn't give her seat to a white person? Were white people free to sit where they wanted? Was Rosa free to sit where she wanted? What did Martin say? Do you think people listened?

Martin said that all people—whether black or white—should be allowed to sit where they wanted on the bus. Martin also used his strong voice to convince many people not to ride the bus until all black people were allowed to sit anywhere. Martin started a bus boycott.

Martin started to get blacks together.

Martin said, "We will not get on the buses."

Martin's boycott worked. Soon the buses were nearly empty, and the bus company began to lose money. Some people were becoming very angry with Martin.

CHAPTER 4
The Buses

Martin Luther King said, "We are not free. We cannot be free until we can sit on a bus where we want."

Martin Luther King and his friends would not go on the bus. No one would get on the buses.

Martin Luther King was a great leader. He said, "We are not mad, but we will be treated well. We will not get on the buses until we are free to sit where we want."

Then Martin and others sang songs. Martin and his friends were strong.

What was Martin Luther King's dream?

CHAPTER 5
Martin Wins the Nobel Peace Prize

The bus boycott went well. People walked to work. People with cars gave others rides, and the buses stood empty. This made some white people mad, so Martin Luther King was arrested. This was very wrong!

Martin Luther King said, "I will not get mad. We will be strong."

Many people thought Martin Luther King was right about the buses. Finally, the courts said that Martin was right.

Martin Luther King said, "We are free! We are free to sit on the buses where we want."

Martin Luther King's dream became real. Now all people can sit where they want.

Martin Luther King wanted people of all colors to be treated equally. Next Martin organized a sit-in. He and his black friends went to a lunch counter that said, "Whites Only."

Martin said, "I do not understand why we cannot eat where we want." Then Martin and his friends went to eat where blacks were not wanted. Martin said, "Let us eat."

The man said, "Go! Go!"

Martin and his friends sat and sang. When others got mad, Martin did not grumble. He said, "We should all eat together."

Again, Martin Luther King was arrested, and again he won in the courts. The laws said that all people were to be treated equally. Martin Luther King won the Nobel Peace Prize for his efforts to make our lives better.

Sadly, Martin Luther King was shot and killed one day. Still, his words were so strong and his work is so important that we honor him today with a national holiday—Martin Luther King Day. We will not forget Martin Luther King. He is a hero.

Why won't we forget Martin Luther King? When people got mad at Martin, did he get into fights? He used his words and peaceful actions to get people to treat others well.

free   freedom

CHAPTER 6

Freedom Rings

When Martin Luther King was shot, it was sad. We lost a great, great man.

We can't meet Martin Luther King, but we can still listen to his dreams. If Martin Luther King were still with us, he would tell us to treat others well.

He would say:

Let us stand together.

Let us dream together.

Let us work together.

Let us be brothers and sisters.

We can remember what Martin
Luther King did. We can remember his
dreams. We can work on his dreams.

Let freedom ring.

How are the children on this page remembering Martin Luther King's dreams?

Martin Luther King's Accomplishments

In "Let Freedom Ring" we learned about Martin Luther King. How did Martin Luther King think all people should be treated?

Look at the pictures below.
Tell me about the pictures.
Start your sentence by saying,
"Now people of all colors . . . "

Storybook Decoding Review

■ **Sounds you know:**

er	G	th	u	ea
f	ar	b	o	⁻y
i	e	F	er	W

▲ **Words you can sound out:**

under	soon	why	thing
get	must	free	going
little	start	better	being

✈ **Words you have learned:**

legs	work	word	school
go	about	friend	were

✿ **Phrases you can read:**

my other friend	the smallest one
after a rest	brother and sister

✎ **Sentences you can read:**

Mother went with us because we asked her.

"What's the matter?" asked Bill.

Bell did not understand about school.